FEB 2 0 199	DATE DUE		
JUL 8 199			
AUG 13 1991			
AUG 30 1991			
JUN. 9 1992			
OCT 7 1992			
MAY 1 3 '96			
AUG 1 3			
JY 2 3 '14			

CENTER STAGE

HULK HOGAN

By
William Sanford
Carl Green

Edited By
Dr. Howard Schroeder
Professor in Reading and Language Arts
Dept. of Elementary Education
Mankato State University

Produced & Designed By
Baker Street Productions, Ltd.

CRESTWOOD HOUSE
Mankato, Minnesota
U.S.A.

LIBRARY OF CONGRESS CATALOGING IN PUBLICATION DATA

Sanford, William R. (William Reynolds), 1927 -
  Hulk Hogan

  (Center stage)
  SUMMARY: A brief biography of the well-known professional wrestler.
  1. Hogan, Hulk, 1955-   —Juvenile literature. 2. Wrestlers—United States—
Biography—Juvenile Literature. [1. Hogan, Hulk, 1955-   . 2. Wrestlers] I. Green,
Carl R. II Schroeder, Howard. III .Title. IV. Series.
GV1196.H64S26   1986   796.8'12'0924 [B] [92]   86-13381
ISBN 0-89686-299-2

International Standard
Book Number:
0-89686-299-2

Library of Congress
Catalog Card Number:
86-13381

ILLUSTRATION CREDITS:

Cover: Nick Elgar/LGI
Boris Smith/LGI: 5
UPI/Bettmann Newsphotos: 6
Harold Stucker/LGI: 9, 13
Nick Elgar/LGI: 10, 14, 24, 28
Lynn Goldsmith: 16
Stephen Crichlow/LGI: 19
AP/Wide World Photos: 20, 27, 30
Boris Smith/LGI: 23

Hwy. 66 South, Box 3427
Mankato, MN 56002-3427
507-388-1616

TABLE
OF
CONTENTS

INTRODUCTION

Let's hear it for Hulkamania!

In a small town, Saturday afternoon is often the time when people go shopping. This Saturday is different in Centerville, U.S.A.

Main Street is quiet, almost ghostly. Everyone has driven out to the Sports Palace at the edge of town. Dusty pickup trucks fill the parking lot. Families stand in line to buy tickets. Little kids run around, trying to knock each other down.

At one o'clock, the doors open. The speakers blast out some lively rock music. A man stands in the center of a raised ring with a microphone in his hand. "Live! From Madison Square Garden in New York City!" he yells. "We're proud to bring WrestleMania to Centerville!"

A spotlight snaps on. Everyone looks at the door to the dressing rooms. A blond giant of a man steps into the bright light. The crowd goes wild. This is their hero, the World Champion! Hulk Hogan waves to his fans as he enters the ring. A moment later, his opponent marches in. Nikolai Volkoff is carrying a Russian flag.

Fans love their World Champion wrestler, Hulk Hogan!

The crowd boos. "The Hulkster will kill you!" a woman yells.

The crowd settles down to watch the match. The fans know that Hogan and Volkoff will put on a good show. The bell rings and the two men circle each other. Suddenly, Volkoff grabs Hogan and flips him over the ropes. Hogan seems stunned. Can he recover? Can he hold on to his championship?

The Hulkster can't be beaten. After forty minutes of rowdy action, he pins the Russian. The crowd cheers wildly. It's clear that Hulk Hogan is the biggest name in wrestling. Experts say that WrestleMania should really be named Hulkamania.

Hulk Hogan is the biggest name in wrestling.

From Centerville to New York, wrestling is a hot ticket these days. In the cities, fans pay up to $200 (US) for ringside seats. Television carries the matches across the U.S. and to many other countries. Hulk Hogan wrestling videos, T-shirts, sweatbands, and dolls sell out in the stores. Wrestling has come a long way from its beginnings in ancient times.

CHAPTER ONE

An ancient sport

Pictures of wrestlers can be seen on the pottery of ancient Egypt and Greece. The drawings prove that wrestling is over three thousand years old. Not only is wrestling a very old sport, it is one of the simplest. Wrestlers grab their opponents and try to throw them to the ground. To be a wrestler requires strength, agility, and courage. But you don't need costly equipment or fancy playing fields.

Wrestling was a popular sport in the early Olympic Games. The Greek wrestlers won their matches by "pinning" their opponents' shoulders to the ground. Rules were written to prevent unfair moves and holds. During the match, a referee kept the match fair and watched for the pin.

Amateur wrestling remains "pure"

Over the centuries, wrestling went in two different directions. Amateur wrestling developed in the spirit of the Greeks. Amateurs wrestle for the love of the sport. Professional wrestling, on the other hand, is more of a show than it is a sport. Professionals are paid to entertain the audience.

Amateur wrestlers fight on thick mats, without any ropes to mark the edges. Professionals, by contrast, wrestle in a boxing ring. The biggest difference, however is the rules. Referees strictly enforce the amateur rules. No hold is legal if its only purpose is to cause pain. Amateur wrestlers may not choke each other, nor may they butt with their heads. Body slams are allowed only if the wrestlers keep one knee on the mat.

Amateur wrestling rules vary from place to place. Under American college rules, wrestlers win a "fall" when they pin opponents to the mat for two seconds. In the Olympics, wrestlers win a fall as soon as their opponents' shoulders touch the mat. In Europe, Greco-Roman wrestlers must make all their holds above the waist. They cannot use their legs for tripping or holding. The Japanese have their own style of wrestling, called sumo. Sumo wrestlers win by shoving their opponents out of the ring.

Professional wrestling is good theater

Professional wrestlers have been around for a long time. As a young man, Abraham Lincoln earned $10

(US) for winning a match. Wrestling drew crowds at carnivals and country fairs, but it was never a big moneymaker. That all changed when wrestling and television found each other in the 1950's. Television needed exciting programs, and professional wrestlers needed an audience. The wrestlers learned to "hype" their matches to build up interest. Gorgeous George, for example, sprayed himself with perfume before he wrestled.

A professional match can last up to an hour. Once the match begins, "anything goes." The referees pretend to enforce the rules, but the wrestlers usually ignore them. Their job is to entertain the fans by doing terrible things to each other. In most matches, one wrestler plays the "good guy" and the other wrestler is the "bad guy." A few wrestlers are so wild they're called "crazies."

Terry caught on quickly to the tricks of wrestling.

The audiences love to cheer their heroes and boo the villains. Some fans are rich and some are poor, but they all agree on one thing: other sports have too many rules. At a wrestling match, people let themselves go. They yell and throw ice at the wrestlers. Anything can happen. As one writer says, ''What other sport lets you kick a guy when he's down?''

The audience loves to be entertained by Hulk Hogan.

It's all in the script

The wrestlers know who will win before the match begins. They follow a "script" written by the promoters. After all, the fans don't come to see Hulk Hogan lose. But it wouldn't be much fun if the match was one-sided. So the Hulk always comes close to losing. Just when it looks as though the bad guy will pin him, the Hulk gains new energy. He roars back with an atomic knee drop to win the match.

Watching Hulk Hogan in action is like watching a movie star do his own stunts. The Hulk is a super athlete. Somehow, he has to pin his opponents without actually injuring them—and without being injured himself. After all, a serious injury could end a career. For the Hulk, that would mean losing a million dollars (US) a year.

With so much money to be made, wrestling has changed. Critics complain that today's wrestlers do more talking than wrestling. The public doesn't seem to mind. Twenty-five million fans tune in every week on cable TV. Perhaps a few of them believe that professional wrestling really is a sport. But there are also folks who believe in the tooth fairy!

What does Hulk Hogan think? He's having the time of his life.

CHAPTER TWO

The kid from Muscle Beach

Hulk Hogan was born in Venice Beach, California, in 1955. At birth, his name was Terry Jean Bollette. When he was growing up, Terry was interested in rock music and body building. Venice was a good place for both. Hollywood's music industry was only a few miles away. Closer to home, weight lifters worked out on the Venice beaches. The wide strip of sand was widely known as Muscle Beach.

Terry learned to play the bass guitar. Before long, he was good enough to play in local rock bands. Between jobs, Terry started lifting weights. "Pumping iron," as the weight lifters called it, paid off. When Terry flexed, his muscles moved like snakes under his skin! He looked at his huge biceps and called them "pythons." By then he had grown to a height of 6'8" (203 cm) and a weight of three hundred pounds (136 kg). Terry's size and muscular good looks made people look twice when he walked by.

Exit Terry, enter Sterling

By 1976, Terry was bored with his lifestyle. He wanted a more exciting career. That's when he met up with Freddie Blassie. Blassie told Terry that he could make it as a professional wrestler. That sounded good to Terry. He had wanted to be a wrestler ever since his dad took him to see his first match.

Blassie started training Terry for the life of a wrestler. It wasn't enough to be strong. Terry had to learn how to fall and how to take a punch. He caught on quickly to the tricks of the trade. Falling out of the ring and

One of the "bad guys" has Hogan down.

being hit with a folding chair were all in a day's work.

After six months of training, Terry was ready. But all of Blassie's wrestlers were bad guys. That meant Terry had to become a "heel," as the bad guys call themselves. He took the name of Sterling Golden and joined the wrestling tour.

People took one look at the tanned blond giant and didn't know what to think. Sterling was too handsome and too likeable to be a heel. Many fans refused to boo him. Sterling kept his mouth shut and did his best to be a good bad guy. Later, looking back on this time, he said, "I was a young kid, lost and misguided."

Sterling was too likeable to be a "bad guy" for long.

Hulk Hogan is born

Hulk Hogan was born in 1982, thanks to Hollywood. Sylvester Stallone was making the third *Rocky* movie. In *Rocky III*, he wrote a scene in which Rocky Balboa loses to a huge wrestler. The scene was based on a real event: Muhammed Ali, a heavyweight boxing champion, once lost to a wrestler—the well-named Gorilla Monsoon. Stallone hired Sterling for this part. Sterling changed his name to Hulk Hogan. The Hulk played a wrestler named Thunderlips in *Rocky III*.

The film made Hulk Hogan a star. People started following him around, asking for autographs. Vince McMahon, Jr., the head of the World Wrestling Federation (WWF), bought up the Hulk's contract. Vince looked at the Hulk's blond good looks and twenty-four inch (61 cm) biceps. He decided that the Hulk had the stuff to be a world champion wrestler.

Vince started the Hulk's new career by dressing him in a bright red T-shirt. The lettering across the chest read, "American Made." Bad guy Sterling Golden was gone. Hulk Hogan now stood for all that was good about this country. When he wrestled, he carried America's hopes against the forces of evil.

There wasn't any doubt about it. Cheering for the Hulkster, as people call him, was as American as apple pie. Whenever the Hulk wrestled, it was standing room only. But was he good enough to win the world championship?

15

CHAPTER THREE

Hulkamania begins

Hulk Hogan quickly became a regular on the WWF's television shows. Here was a true-blue American hero! Fans went crazy when the Hulk stepped into the ring.

Hulkamania was born. As the Hulk says, "What's it all about? I'll tell you what Hulkamania is all about. . . . Brother, you got to live it, you got to experience it. You got to have it flow in your blood before you can even come close to believing in it."

Hogan shows some of his championship form!

A few critics refused to jump on the Hulkster's bandwagon. Sure, he turns on the crowd, they said, but he's not a very good wrestler. The Hulk doesn't know enough holds, one writer complained. In addition, former champion Bob Backlund was angry that the Hulk got his title shot so quickly. "Hogan doesn't deserve a shot as much as the guy who's proved himself for the last five years," Backlund said.

On his way to a title match

As long as Hulk was selling tickets, no one listened to the critics. And did he sell tickets! The WWF put him into as many as ten matches a week. Some matches were held in television studios, but most took place in front of live audiences. A cheering, screaming crowd adds a lot to a wrestling match. The Hulk quickly earned his title fight. In January, 1984, he came to Madison Square Garden in New York City to fight for the world championship.

In the twenty-year history of the WWF, only eight wrestlers had worn the champion's gold belt. Bob Backlund held the title for almost six years. He lost it to the Iron Sheik in December, 1983. The Sheik played the role of a truly rotten bad guy. The fans would like it if someone like the Hulk could take the championship away from him.

Over twenty thousand people packed Madison Square Garden for the match. The Iron Sheik entered the ring first. He was dressed like an Iranian desert nomad. Then the crowd jumped to its feet. *Eye of the Tiger* blared out over the loudspeakers. This music from *Rocky III* was the Hulk's theme song. Hogan wore his "American Made" T-shirt. The message was clear. This was good against evil.

Escaping the Camel Clutch

The Hulk didn't wait for the bell. He grabbed the Iron Sheik's headdress and tried to choke him with it. The referee got them separated. A little later, the Hulk missed a flying body block. He slammed into the padded buckle at the corner of the ring. The Sheik saw his chance. He sat on the Hulk's back and pulled upward on the Hulkster's chin. The crowd gasped. The Hulk was caught in the Sheik's Camel Clutch. No one had ever escaped from this deadly hold!

Slowly, the Hulkster came back to life. The fans shouted, "Hogan! Hogan!" He rose to one knee. The Sheik held onto his punishing hold. The Hulk stood up! The Sheik was now hanging helplessly from the Hulk's back. The Hulk sprang backward and smashed the Sheik against the corner of the ring. The Sheik dropped to the floor.

Hulk gets ready to smash his opponent.

The Hulk bounced off the ropes to build up speed. The Sheik was trying to stand up when the flying Hulk hit him in the neck with his elbow. The champion dropped to the mat. Before he could get up, the Hulk flattened him for the pin. The referee counted to three. Hulk Hogan was the new WWF champion!

The *Eye of the Tiger* was played again and again. The Hulk put on the gold championship belt. Then he did a victory dance, flexing his "pythons." The crowd chanted, "U.S.A.! U.S.A.!" Hulk Hogan was riding high on a new surge of Hulkamania.

The Hulk says that you've got to experience "Hulkamania" to believe it!

CHAPTER FOUR

The show biz connection

With Hulk Hogan as champion, wrestling kept on growing. Show business stars showed up to join in the fun. Rock singer Cyndi Lauper came to a match to give a platinum record to the WWF. The Hulk was there. So was Cyndi's manager, Dave Wolff.

Everything was peaceful until Rowdy Roddy Piper turned up. Rowdy Roddy was the bad guy in the script. He smashed the record and bodyslammed Dave Wolff to the mat. Cyndi jumped into the ring to help Dave. Roddy kicked her in the face. That was too much for the Hulk. He slugged Rowdy Roddy. Mr. T, star of television's *A Team*, ran up to help the Hulk. The police arrived just in time to prevent a riot.

The near-riot set the stage for a revenge battle. The Hulk and Mr. T challenged Roddy and Paul "Mr. Wonderful" Orndorff to a tag-team match. In a tag match, only two wrestlers fight at a time. Their partners wait in neutral corners. If the Hulk is wrestling and he gets tired or hurt, he "tags" Mr. T. Fresh and strong, Mr. T then takes the Hulk's place in the ring.

21

WrestleMania puts on a wild show

The WWF called this special match WrestleMania. It turned into one of Madison Square Garden's biggest shows. Ringside tickets sold for $100 (US). Liberace, the famous piano player, was timekeeper. Baseball manager Billy Martin was the ring announcer, and the referee was Muhammed Ali. The promoters even hired four dancers from the Radio City Rockettes.

Everyone had something to say about the match. Cyndi Lauper told people that it was "the brawl to settle it all." The Hulkster warned the bad guys that he and Mr. T were going to whip them. Mr. T added, "We are the dream team." *Ms.* magazine editor Gloria Steinem laughed at the Scotch kilts that Rowdy Roddy wears. "He's not fit to wear a skirt!" she said.

Finally, the big night came. The crowd enjoyed the early matches, but everyone was waiting for the main event. Finally, Rowdy Roddy and Mr. Wonderful entered behind twenty bagpipers. The crowd booed both of them. Then *Eye of the Tiger* sounded. The Hulk and Mr. T bounded into the ring. The Garden rocked with the shouts and screams of Hulkamania!

The "dream team" in action

Mr. Wonderful squared off against the Hulk, but Roddy soon took his place. The Hulk tagged Mr. T,

Mr. T and the Hulk get ready to take on Mr. Wonderful and Rowdy Roddy.

Muhammed Ali, Liberace, and the Hulk posed for a picture before the match in Madison Square Garden.

who traded slaps with Roddy. All at once, Roddy put Mr. T down with some hard body chops. Mr. T fought back. He slammed Roddy to the mat. With that, Mr. Wonderful attacked Mr. T from behind. The Hulk joined in. Soon all four wrestlers were throwing punches. Roddy gouged the Hulk's face with his thumbs. Security guards finally pulled the four angry men apart.

Roddy took a swing at Muhammed Ali. That was a mistake. The former champion still has a wicked punch.

He chased Roddy out of the ring. Roddy and Mr. Wonderful said the referee was against them. They headed for their dressing room. Ali began counting them out. If he reached ten, the match would be over. The Hulk stopped the count and dared the two heels to return. Roddy and his partner took the dare. Their pride was on the line.

A surprise ending

The Hulk soon had both bad guys in the ring at the same time. He banged their heads together. Then he kicked Roddy out of the ring and went after him. Roddy hit him with a folding chair. Back in the ring, Mr. T took over. Roddy came back and began stomping on him. Mr. T was barely able to tag Hulk.

Roddy and Mr. Wonderful were on a roll. They put a double Atomic Spinebreaker on the Hulk. While Ali was warning them that the hold was illegal, one of Roddy's friends sneaked into the ring. Cowboy Bob Orton's plan was to hit the Hulk with his plaster cast. But just as he swung, the alert Hulkster stepped aside. The Cowboy's cast knocked Mr. Wonderful down and out. The Hulk then jumped on his dazed opponent for an easy pin.

The match was over. The Hulk and Mr. T put on a flashy victory dance. The good guys had won again.

CHAPTER FIVE

Good words from the Hulkster

Hulk Hogan enjoys being a star. It makes him feel good when people scream his name. He likes to talk to his fans and to sign autographs. Their love is important to him.

"Before I was a wrestler, my sense of self-respect was zero," he explains. "I couldn't help myself or anybody that I loved. Then I suddenly became a mat star and . . . I was cheered for doing what I do best. . . . It never ceases to astonish me that meeting me can make a sick child feel better. That's a gift more precious than any wrestling title in the world."

Talking about Hulkamania really turns him on. "Hulkamania is about getting your act together," the Hulk tells his young fans. He calls them his "little Hulksters." He flexes his big arms and says, "[Hulkamania] is getting rid of those puny chicken-wing arms. It's getting into the gym for some heavy-duty weight training. But along with that, you have to say your prayers and eat your vitamins. . . . Everything you do has to be real positive. . . . I fear no man and no evil once I have the people on my side."

"I fear no man and no evil once I have the people on my side,"
says the Hulkster.

The Hulk visits with a young fan.

The Hulk also takes his message to children in hospitals. They love it when he says, "If you work hard and get to bed early you can accomplish anything. And I mean anything, Daddy!" If they're lucky, he gives them a glass of Hulkster's Choice Milk. The Hulk calls this mixture "the breakfast of body slammers."

Young or old, wrestling fans can't get enough of their hero. His records, which feature the Hulkster on bass guitar, are number one sellers in Japan. In the United States, little Hulksters watch a cartoon show called *Hulk Hogan's Rock 'n' Wrestling*. Their parents buy wrestling videos that feature the Hulk. And people everywhere seem to be buying Hulkster sweatbands and T-shirts.

It's not easy being the Hulk

The Hulk says that wrestling is everything to him. "There's nothing better than eating right, getting a pump on and then going out and facing the best in the world . . . and winning." He knows that the other wrestlers want to take his title away. "Every time you step into the combat zone you take a chance on your life," he explains. "You have to run to be bigger and better than you were last time, or you're doomed."

Some wrestlers are bigger, but no one is better. In 1985, *Wrestling Eye* magazine gave the Hulk his highest honor. The editor named him "Wrestler of the Year."

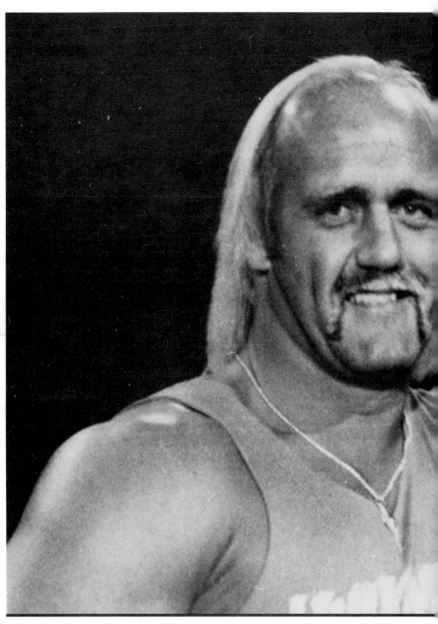

In 1985, Wrestling Eye *named Hogan "Wrestler of the Year."*
The Hulkster isn't ready to retire yet!

Other magazines haven't been as kind. The Hulk doesn't get upset at articles that call him a monster, however. "I take monster as a compliment," he says with a smile. "It doesn't mean something ugly to me. It means I can't be stopped. It means even other wrestlers can't believe how big I am. I'm rich and famous. If that's an oddity, I want more."

The future looks good

Hulk Hogan has been wrestling for over ten years. He knows it will all end someday. "The only thing that scares me is retirement," he admits. He loves being the world champion.

Who's going to tell Hulk Hogan that it's time to quit? Plenty of wrestlers would like to end his career. Will it be someone like Big John Studd, the Junkyard Dog, or Sgt. Slaughter?

The Hulk says that any of them would be good champions. "But first, they have to take the belt away from me," he adds. With that, he jumps back into the ring. He rips off his T-shirt and shakes his blond hair. Then he flexes, and his muscles move like coiling snakes. Twenty thousand fans are on their feet. "Hogan! Hogan!" they scream.

Hulkamania is alive and well.